This is the end.
We hope you enjoyed this book.

Peter Eldin

The Complete
Practical Joker

Illustrated by Phil Emms

SPARROW
BOOKS

A Sparrow Book

Published by
Arrow Books Limited
3 Fitzroy Square, London W1P 6JD

An imprint of the Hutchinson Publishing Group

London Melbourne Sydney Auckland
Wellington Johannesburg and agencies
throughout the world

First published 1981
© Eldin Editorial Services 1981

Set in Linoterm Times Roman by
Rowland Phototypesetting Ltd
Bury St Edmunds, Suffolk

Made and printed in Great Britain
by The Anchor Press Ltd
Tiptree, Essex

Rules for Practical Jokers

Try to pick your victims with care. A lot of people like to see jokes played on other people, but they can quickly lose their own sense of humour when the joke is played on them.

Do not use a practical joke if it is not funny. True, it may not appear funny to the victim at the time, but if it makes you and others laugh *and it is harmless* then you can be reasonably safe in using it.

Never use a practical joke in anger or out of spite. Practical jokes should be done for fun – not to hurt someone.

Always wear running shoes when perpetrating a prank. You will be able to run away much faster.

Never use a practical joke that might cause injury to someone.

Never use a joke that might really upset someone. It can be quite funny to hand someone a wriggling worm when they least expect it. But if that person is genuinely scared of worms then you should not do anything like this to them.

If a joke is messy – like the jammy handshake on page 40 – do not play it on someone who is wearing their best clothes. Apart from being rather unfair you may not appreciate the joke when you have to pay for the clothes to be cleaned.

Never play practical jokes on elderly people.

Do not worry if you are not actually on the scene when the victim is caught. It can be just as much fun to imagine what happened when the target fell for your trick.

Never own up to being a practical joker – that is part of the fun.

Do try to enjoy the joke if you are the target for a change. You should be able to take it as well as give it.

If you get caught doing any of the pranks described in this book, don't blame me. I will have left the country long before then.

Smudge

Put some of your mum's lipstick on the tips of the first two fingers of your right hand.

While talking to a friend suddenly say: 'Oh, you've got a smudge on your face'. He will try to wipe it off but you insist that it is still there. 'Come here, I will wipe it off for you', you say. But your offer is not so considerate as it sounds for you use your first two fingers to wipe off the imaginary smudge.

Everybody will have a good laugh at your friend's expense for he now has a lovely red mark on his face, thanks to you!

Philately Will Get You Nowhere

You ask a friend: 'Do you collect stamps?'

If he replies: 'Yes, I do,' stamp on his foot and say: 'Well, there's one for your collection!'

If he says: 'No,' you still stamp on his foot but you say: 'Well, there's one to start you off!'

Please do not stamp on your friend's foot too hard. It is meant to be a joke!

It Really Happened . . .

At seven o'clock one evening in May 1947 the American Armed Forces Radio Station in Tokyo, Japan, interrupted its programme with a report that a twenty-foot-long sea monster had come ashore near to the city.

Every five minutes they gave further bulletins. The monster was approaching the city and causing havoc on the way. Eventually the armed forces tried to stop the monster before it reached the city – but to no avail. Even flame throwers could not stop this ferocious beast.

Another report stated that the creature had attacked a train leaving the city. The train had been derailed but no one dared to check on the number of injured.

The reports sounded so genuine that a great number of people were taken in by them. These included the military police and the army who mobilized their troops to deal with the approaching menace. But at eight o'clock the radio announcer owned up. The whole story had been a joke!

Mental Arithmetic

Tell your friends that you are a great mind-reader. Say that you are so great that if they do some mental arithmetic you can easily call out the answer.

Ask your victim to think of any small number. He is then to double it, add seven, and then take away the number he first thought of. Say: 'As I said before, I am the world's greatest mind-reader. Even though I could not possibly know the first number you thought of I have followed all the calculations you made in your head and I can now call out the answer.' And that is exactly what you do. You call out: 'The answer!'

Now get ready to run away.

The Eggcellent Cook

Next time you have some friends for tea, offer to let them try your delicious boiled eggs. When you go into the kitchen you put into the egg cups the empty shells of the eggs you and your family had for breakfast that morning. The tops and bottoms of these shells have been glued together so that the shells are complete.

When your friends open their eggs they find absolutely nothing inside!

If you are a particularly horrible type of practical joker you could fill the egg shells with wet, gooey mud before gluing them together. Ugh!

Walking Pound Note

With a piece of sticky tape fix one end of a length of cotton to a £1 note. (You have to be rich for this practical joke!)

Put the money on the pavement. You hide behind a nearby bush with the other end of the cotton.

Now all you do is wait. Sooner or later someone will come along and spot the money. As the person reaches down to pick up the cash you pull the thread – and the money leaps away from the persons outstretched hand!

As well as being rich you also have to be quick for this trick. If your victim's reactions are quicker than yours he or she will grab the money before you can whip it away and you will be the loser!

It Really Happened . . .

Among the many exhibits to be seen in the Royal Scottish Museum, Edinburgh, are some rather amazing creatures. Among the stuffed birds there is one species unknown to naturalists. It has the head of a crow, the body of a plover, and the wings and tail-feathers are those of a duck! Even if this strange combination of features does not make you suspicious, and the fact that the bird has a magnificent frontage of what appears to be red wax does not strike you as peculiar, the name of the bird ought to convince you that the bird is a fake. It is called the 'Bare-faced Hoodwink'.

Bouncing Handkerchief

Get a small rubber ball and sew it in the centre of a handkerchief. The easiest way to do this is to get someone else to do it for you! If you have to do it yourself simply hold all four corners of the handkerchief together, drop the ball inside the bag you have formed and then sew the material together just above the ball. The sewing does not have to be anything fancy, provided that it is good enough to hold the ball in position.

When you are with some friends take the special handkerchief from your pocket to blow your nose. Then throw the handkerchief on the floor – and it bounces right back up again!

Casually put the handkerchief back in your pocket taking no notice of the astonished looks on the faces of all your friends.

The Monster

Remove the greaseproof bag from an empty cereal packet. Now all you have to do is catch a fly – and that is not as easy as it sounds! Put the fly in the bag and screw the top up slightly so it cannot escape.

Tell your friend that you have a terrible monster in the bag. Ask him to tilt his head to one side and then you hold the bag against his ear. Surprising as it may seem, the movements of the fly inside the bag really do sound as if you have a monster in there.

The Magic Pen

You tell your intended victim that you are a great mind-reader and that you are able to reproduce anything he writes with your pen even though you do not see what has been written. You then hand him your pen and a piece of paper and ask him to write something – anything he likes.

As he takes the pen and paper you repeat what you said before. 'Anything you write with that pen I will be able to write on another piece of paper even though I do not see what has been written.'

Now get ready to run, for it will be at about this point that your friend will discover the truth of your claim – because he cannot write anything at all with the pen! Crafty joker that you are, you removed the ink cartridge before you gave it to him!

The Practical Joker's Favourite Day

The favourite day of the year for all practical jokers is 1 April when you can get away with anything – almost! There are many possible explanations of why 1 April is known as All Fools' Day and no one seems to know for certain which is correct. One suggestion is that the custom dates back to the time of Noah; another theory is that it is a survival of a Roman Festival, Cerealia, which was held at the beginning of April.

In India, during the Huli Festival on 31 March, people play tricks on one another, so it is possible that the custom may have come from the East. The most popular theory is that it represents the last remnants of the celebrations that centuries ago marked the start of the New Year, for during the Middle Ages 25 March was New Year's Day.

In 1564 the French adopted the Gregorian Calendar that we use today and New Year's Day became 1 January. People took a long time to get used to the new calendar and hoaxers added to the confusion by playing jokes on their friends on 1 April. The custom crossed the Channel in 1752 when Britain changed to the Gregorian Calendar.

In France an April Fool is called *un poisson d'Avril* (an April fish).

17

Your Wheel is Going Round

As a friend cycles by, point anxiously at the front wheel of his bike and shout: 'Your front wheel is going round!'

It is an old joke, but you will be surprised at the number of people who will get off their bike to check that the wheel is all right!

The Great Yawn

Have you ever noticed that yawning is catching? If someone keeps yawning you can bet your life that it will not be very long before you too have your mouth wide open in an enormous yawn. You can use this fact for a neat practical joke.

Whenever you are in a crowd of people at a party, on a bus, or in the doctor's waiting room have a great big yawn. Every so often repeat your yawn. And other people around you will begin to yawn – but none of them know why. You do.

Coin Popper

Place a coin on top of an empty lemonade bottle. Now tell your friends that you can make the coin move purely by concentrating your incredible bionic brain.

They will not believe you until they see you start to concentrate and the coin begins to jump up and down on top of the bottle.

The secret of this little stunt has, of course, got nothing to do with the power of your brain – even if it is bionic! All you have to do is to place the coin on top of the bottle with a wet finger. Run the finger around the edge of the coin so the water makes an effective seal.

Now hold the bottle in both hands. The heat from your hands will warm the air inside the bottle. As the air expands it forces its way out of the bottle and causes the coin to pop up and down.

On many occasions you will find that the coin continues to pop up and down even after you have let go of the bottle.

It Really Happened . . .

In 1977 the *Guardian* newspaper published a seven-page special report about the island republic of San Serriffe. On the surface the report appeared genuine for it contained advertisements congratulating the republic on the occasion of its tenth year of independence and a profile of the republic's president General Maria-Jesu Pica. Only a few of the paper's readers realized that the whole report was an enormous hoax and that the name of the republic and that of its president were in fact printing terms.

Rude Balloon

Blow up balloon. Now place the forefinger and thumb of each hand on either side of the neck. By pulling the neck taut and releasing some of the air from the balloon you can make quite a variety of different noises.

Do this secretly on a bus, in a queue, or even while walking down the street and watch the reactions of people near you. They can be most funny.

Money for Nothing

Most people would welcome the chance to get some money for nothing, and in this prank you appear to offer them the chance.

Show your friend an empty matchbox. Now put a ten pence coin into the box and close it. Rattle the box to prove that the coin really is in it.

Open the box again and ask your friend to put another ten pence in. Again close the box and rattle the coins in it. Place the box on the table and ask: 'How much is in the box?' To this question your friend will naturally reply: 'Twenty pence.'

You then say: 'You can buy a lot of sweets with twenty pence. Would you like to make some money?' The reply will invariably be yes. And then you say: 'There is twenty pence in the box. Would you be prepared to give me fifteen pence for it?'

You will be surprised at how many people will be happy to take you up on your offer. They seem to forget that half of the twenty pence was theirs to start with – and you end up with five-pence profit!

23

It Really Happened . . .
Upside-down Room

One of the favourite pranks of the wealthy American practical joker Rudolph Schenk was played on strangers he met in the street. He would invite the stranger to his home where he would be treated to a slap-up meal and a great deal to drink. Eventually the victim would become so drunk that Schenk insisted that he stay the night. Faced with such a charming host and pleasant hospitality the guest seldom refused the offer.

When the stranger fell asleep Schenk would have him gently transferred to a special room he had constructed. When the victim awoke the following morning he received quite a shock – he was hanging from the ceiling! Schenk derived great amusement from watching the antics of his bewildered guest through secret peepholes. The floor of the room had been painted white to look like a ceiling with a chandelier rising from it. The real ceiling was stained to look like floor boards and furniture was affixed to it. As there were no windows in the room the poor victim really thought he was upside down! It must have been quite a relief when Schenk eventually made an appearance and explained that the visitor had been the victim of a practical joke.

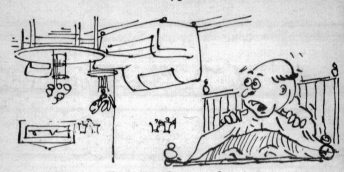

Errands

This must be the oldest practical joke in this book. It is very likely the oldest practical joke in the world. All you have to do is to ask a friend to do an errand for you. When they say they will, you give them some impossible thing to obtain from the local shop such as a gallon of tartan paint, a left-handed screwdriver, or a packet of hot ice cream. See if you can think up some other equally strange items.

With a bit of luck your victim will go off quite happily to get the item you want. But he may not be quite so happy when he finds out he has been tricked.

Cupboard Love

This joke requires a lot of patience. When your victim is out of the room hide yourself in a cupboard or behind a piece of furniture. If someone comes into the room do not make a sound but let them settle down normally.

When you can stand the suspense no longer start making some ghostly moans and watch your victim's hair stand on end!

If you are in a cupboard always take the precaution of wedging something in the door – or your victim may turn the tables on you and shut you in!

Hot Sandwich

Next time you make a sandwich for a friend pop in a small piece of a chilli pepper, some chilli powder, mustard seeds, or a drop or two of tabasco sauce. Have a glass of water handy, for when your friend bites into the delicious sandwich he will think his mouth is on fire when he reaches the hot part!

Do not put too much of the hot substance in the sandwich – just enough to make it nice and hot. It might be a good idea to try it on yourself first so you know what is involved.

It Really Happened . . .

Possibly the most famous hoax of all time was that of Piltdown Man. In 1912 the skull and jaw of what was thought to be the missing link, the long-searched-for connection between ape and man, were discovered at Piltdown, Sussex, England. Later several other remains were found which supported the fact that the original finds were absolutely genuine. Eventually, enough finds were made to reconstruct an almost complete skull – the skull of a creature that had the brain of a human but the jaw of an ape. This 'missing link' became known as 'Piltdown

Man' although, in fact, the remains were those of a female.

For the next forty years the remains were believed in scientific circles to be absolutely genuine although some doubts had been raised as to their authenticity. But in 1953 new scientific examination of the finds revealed that they were nowhere near as old as had previously been thought and that many had been faked. It was finally announced that Piltdown Man was a hoax from beginning to end.

It is not known for certain who perpetrated this audacious practical joke, but the most likely candidate is Charles Dawson. Dawson, a respected lawyer and amateur palaeontologist, was the man who made all the finds and after his death in 1916 no further discoveries were made. Quite why he pulled this elaborate prank is now difficult to decide. It may be that he sought the fame that such revolutionary discoveries would bring. It is equally possible, however, that he just wanted to pull the legs of all the distinguished scientists who declared that the finds were genuine.

Knocked on the Floor

KNOCK
KNOCK

Next time you are seated at a table having a drink with friends, catch them with this joke.

Tell everyone that you can knock your full glass of orange juice (or whatever it is you are drinking) on the floor without spilling a drop.

To everyone present it is obvious that this cannot be done and they will tell you so in no uncertain terms.

You then prove that anything is possible to a practical joker. You carefully place the glass tumbler on the floor. Then you knock it gently with your knuckles.

You have definitely *knocked* it on the floor and your friends will have a good laugh when they realize how easily they have been fooled.

Time for a Change

About an hour or so before your bedtime go secretly all around the house and change the time on all the clocks. If nine o'clock is your normal bedtime put all the clocks back to six o'clock.

Do not mention anything about time but just carry on your normal activities. Sooner or later your mother will tell you to go to bed whereupon you look up at the clock and protest. 'But mum. It is only six o'clock.' She will not believe you and will probably go into another room to check – but as you have changed all the clocks the one in that room will say six o'clock also.

When your mother begins to realize that something is wrong offer to find out the correct time by telephoning the speaking clock. You make the call but ignore the time that is given. Instead you say as innocently as you can: 'That says that it is six o'clock as well'.

Sooner or later you will be found out, but with a bit of luck you will have gained an hour or two before you are finally sent to bed.

Pyjama Panic

All you need for this nifty trick is a needle and cotton . . . oh, and a pair of your victim's pyjamas! Because you need the pyjamas there will only be certain times when you can do this trick – but they will be well worth waiting for.

When your victim is not looking you sew across the bottom of each trouser leg. At bedtime your victim will be in quite a panic for he will not be able to get his feet into his pyjamas!

If you want to carry this joke a stage further you could even sew up the sleeves of your friend's pyjama jacket. Then he really will get into a bit of a panic when he wants to go to bed!

It Really Happened . . .

The heart-throb of the 1920s, Rudolph Valentino, once walked on stage at a film première wearing pyjamas. He said he had overslept and his appearance shocked many of the women present. But it was all a joke for he was wearing full evening dress underneath his night wear.

RUDOLPH VALENTINO

Sealed-up Socks

This is a variation of the last joke. You will have to do some sewing again but this time you sew across the top of a pair of socks. As you have closed the openings into which your victim is to put his feet he will not be able to get his socks on.

Do not do this joke with girls' stockings or tights as the sewing will damage them.

Take Note

This is a very simple and very old prank. It is, nevertheless, very effective. All you have to do is to write something like 'I am an idiot' on a piece of paper. Fix a piece of sticky tape to the paper so it overlaps the edge and you are ready.

As you approach your intended victim keep the paper well hidden. Pat your victim on the back in friendly greeting. At the same time you make the most of the opportunity and stick the notice on his or her back.

Your victim will be very surprised when people around start to laugh for he will have no idea as to what is causing the amusement.

Here are some suggestions for the notice:

I AM AN IDIOT
KISS ME QUICK
RUNNING IN, PLEASE PASS
KEEP AWAY – MEASLES!

Instead of just sticking notices on your friends you could try sticking one on your dad or your teacher – but do not be surprised if he does not think it very funny.

Magic Marker

Here is a quick little joke that should be in the armoury of every dedicated practical joker.

Take a felt-tipped pen from your pocket and remove the cap. Now ask your victim if you can borrow his handkerchief for a moment. When he hands the handkerchief to you you say: 'The trouble with handkerchiefs is that they all look alike. It is almost impossible to prove that it belongs to you. I will just mark it for you so you will know it is yours.' Before your victim can react you apparently draw a line down the handkerchief with the pen.

What you really do is this. Hold the handkerchief in your left hand and the pen in the right (assuming that you are right-handed). Now bring the handkerchief in front of the pen as if you are going to draw on the handkerchief. As soon as the pen is hidden from view you turn it around and run the non-writing end down the material. From your friend's viewpoint it really looks as if you are drawing on the handkerchief. As the pen comes into view turn it around once again and the illusion is perfect – so perfect that your victim will grab at his handkerchief, thinking that you have ruined it. When he examines it he will get quite a shock for the handkerchief is completely unmarked.

It Really Happened . . .

In 1977 the British radio presenter Simon Bates was responsible for an apparently genuine outside broadcast of the finals of the Miss Radio One Beauty Contest. It was said that the winner came from an uninhabited island near Scotland and that she wore a three-piece swimsuit! The broadcast was made on 1 April!

Money for Free

Show a friend a £1 note (assuming, of course, that you are that rich) and announce that he or she can have the note if they can catch it when you let go of it.

Hold the note at one end and ask your victim to place his finger and thumb on either side of the note. He can be as close as he likes to the note provided that he is not actually touching it.

Now say that you will let go of the note without any warning and that he is to try to catch it between his finger and thumb. To make sure he understands you, repeat what you have just said. 'I am going to let drop the note without any warning. Any time now.' Keep on talking and halfway through a sentence suddenly drop the note. It will take a little while for his senses to realize that the note is moving and by that time it is too late – the note has slipped through his fingers.

If you are scared at the thought that your friend might actually catch the note you can always try it out a few times using just a slip of paper. After a while you will see how effective it is and perhaps you will then be able to pluck up enough courage to use the £1 note. If you are really brave (and very rich) you could even try it with a £5 note.

No Entry

One day, in the most unusually generous mood, offer to make your mother's bed. When she recovers from the shock, assure her that you are simply trying to lessen the burden of her housework and then go upstairs to make the bed.

But you are not quite as mad as your mother might think, for you have a dastardly deed in mind.

This is how you make the bed. Fold a sheet in half and lay it over the top half of the mattress. Fold back part of the top part of the sheet to make room for the pillows. Now tuck the edges of the sheet under the mattress on each side. Put the blankets on the bed and tuck them in as usual.

When your parents go to bed that evening they will manage to get only half-way in. The folded sheet prevents them getting into bed in the proper way!

Watch that your mother does not try the same prank on you the following night!

Jammy Handshake

Hold a blob of jam on the palm of your hand. Now go and shake hands with someone!

This is a bit messy both for you and for your victim, but to see the expression on your friend's face when you shake hands makes it well worth the small discomfort.

It Really Happened . . .

American humorist Edgard Nye and poet James
Whitcomb Riley were on a train journey together when
Nye suddenly said, 'Oh dear, I've lost one of the tickets.'
As the ticket-collector was approaching, he suggested
that Riley hid under the seat or they would have to pay for
the lost ticket.

By the time the ticket-collector reached them Riley was
beneath the seat. Nye took both the tickets from his pocket
and handed them to the collector. 'Two tickets?' queried
the collector. 'Who's the other one for?'

Nye then pointed to Riley hiding under the seat. 'It's
for my friend,' he said. 'He always travels like that!'

Ghostly Floater

This is a good practical joke to try on your parents. Fix a long length of cotton to a sheet of white paper. Use a piece of sticky tape for this.

A short while before bedtime place the paper on something high in your parents' bedroom. The top of the wardrobe is a good place. Now run the thread from the paper under the bedroom door, and into your own room. Make sure that the thread runs free and that there is no danger of breaking something when you pull it.

Wait until your parents go into the bedroom, make a loud, ghostly, moaning noise and then give the thread a short tug. Just enough to pull the paper from its hiding place. The paper will rustle and then it will float gently to the floor. It will give your victims quite a fright!

Rubber Liquorice

Get some thick black rubber from your local hardware store. Now buy a stick of liquorice and cut the rubber so that it looks exactly like the liquorice.

When your friends see you eating the liquorice someone is almost certain to ask for a piece. Give him the rubber liquorice and then watch his face when he tries to bite off a piece!

Spoonful of Nothing

Ask an adult to make a large hole in a plastic teaspoon.

Push the spoon into a bowl of sugar so the hole is concealed. Now offer your friends a cup of tea and have a good laugh when they try to spoon some sugar from the bowl but get nothing!

It Really Happened . . .

One Sunday in April 1860 several people were seen heading for the Tower of London. They were on their way to witness the annual custom of washing the white lions. To gain admittance to this traditional ceremony they had to enter the Tower through the White Gate. When they arrived they found a crowd of people already there – searching for the White Gate. Not even the Yeomen of the Guard, the famous Beefeaters, knew where it was.

As the puzzled crowd scratched their heads in bewilderment the truth suddenly dawned. 'Look at the date on the invitation cards,' said one. 'We are the victims of a practical joke. Today is April the first – All Fools' Day!'

It's a Smasher

Offer to wash up the dishes for your mother. You can always say that you are trying to make up for making the bed as you did in a previous prank.

When you go out into the kitchen you begin to wash up the dishes (you have to make some sacrifices if you wish to be a dedicated practical joker!). As soon as your mother is safely relaxed out of sight you take a large bunch of keys, or a number of small pieces of metal, from your pocket.

Drop the keys on the floor with a crash and shout, 'Oh dear, that's mum's best plate!' It will only be a matter of seconds before your mother comes rushing into the kitchen in a panic thinking that you have broken something!

A Nice Cup of Tea

As your poor mother has had to put up with many of the pranks described in this book why don't you offer to change your joking ways. Get your mum to sit down comfortably. Bring her slippers and a magazine to read. Now offer to make her a lovely cup of tea.

She will think you are very kind when you bring the tea to her. But she will soon realize that you are still a dedicated practical joker when she drinks the tea – you made it with cold water, you little rascal!

It's a Snip

This prank requires some secret preparation beforehand. Get a small piece of material from the centre of a white handkerchief. Bunch the four corners in together and sew them to the end of a piece of flat elastic. The piece of elastic should be about the length of your arm. To the other end of the elastic attach a safety pin.

Pin the safety pin inside your coat near to the armhole. Now push the material down the sleeve. When you put your coat back on the material should be just out of sight, hidden inside your cuff. Now arm yourself with a pair of scissors and you are ready to carry out the prank.

When you see your intended victim approaching pull the material down from your sleeve and hold it hidden in your hand. Ask your victim if his handkerchief is dirty. Whatever he replies you ask to see it. Take the handkerchief from him, holding it by the centre. Now push this centre portion into your fist containing the extra piece of material. Keep the real centre of the handkerchief concealed in your hand and push the extra piece up into view. It should look as if you have simply placed the handkerchief into your hand and pulled the centre up a little. It is a good idea to practise this movement in private a few times before trying it out on someone.

You now say: 'There's some dirt on the centre. But don't worry, I'll get rid of it for you. As you say this you remove the scissors from your pocket and calmly cut through the centre of the handkerchief. At least that is what your friend thinks you have done. All you have really done is cut through the extra piece of material.

As your friend makes a grab for his handkerchief let go of it and at the same time let go of the extra piece of material. The elastic will pull the small piece of material out of sight and up your sleeve.

Angered by the fact that you have cut a hole in his handkerchief your victim will open it out in his temper. But when he does so his rage will turn into bewilderment for his handkerchief is completely unharmed – and you can have a good laugh for he will have no idea how you fooled him.

It Really Happened . . .

A hoaxer had an advertisement printed in a Welsh newspaper a few years ago. It read: 'Lost. One three-humped camel. Owner desperate. Reward.'

The telephone number given was that of a public house, and it was not very long before the publican received a great number of calls from people claiming the reward!

Not so Sweet

In many hardware shops and market stalls it is possible to buy sheets of foam for filling cushions and so on. For this prank you need a very small piece of white foam. As it is so small you may be able to persuade the shopkeeper to let you have it for just a few pence.

Cut the foam into cubes. These cubes must be exactly the same size as a cube of sugar. And now you have probably guessed what is coming next! That's right, you put your foam cubes in a sugar bowl along with some real sugar cubes. Now sit back and watch your victims as they sugar their tea.

If they pick up the sugar with their fingers the foam cubes will compress, much to your victims' amazement. If they use a spoon it is quite likely that they may not notice anything unusual and put the cubes into their tea or coffee – and the cubes will float on the surface of the drink!

Toffee Spuds

Ask your mother to make you some toffee apples. At the same time get her to use potatoes in place of some of the apples. You will, of course, have to make sure that you select potatoes that are more or less the same size and shape as the apples your mother is using.

It is a good idea to use slightly different sticks for the potatoes or to mark them in some way so you know which are which.

When the toffee has set invite your friends around for a treat. Take one of the toffee apples for yourself and offer your friends the ones that contain potatoes. They will get quite a surprise when they bite through the toffee and find a potato instead of a delicious apple!

Pennies from Heaven

This is really only for you if you are prepared to spend some money on your practical jokes. It will not, however, cost you very much. If you are careful how much you spend on this prank you can get a great deal of fun for a relatively modest outlay.

Find a good hiding place near to a public path. You will also need a supply of ½ p coins.

When someone walks by throw a coin so it lands at his feet. In the majority of cases he will stop, look down, and then pick up the coin.

As soon as he starts walking again toss another coin at his feet. This time reactions will vary from person to person and this is where the fun comes in for you. You are, after all is said and done, spending money, so you may as well get as much fun as you can out of the situation. Some people will just pick up the coin as if money falling from the sky is the most natural thing in the world. Others will look around with suspicion. Others may be so scared by the strange occurrence that they will run for their lives! Throughout the whole thing you must do your best not to laugh out loud or you will give the whole game away.

If your target is the type who just picks up the coins without question, do not carry the joke on for too long or you will end up broke!

It Really Happened . . .

The people in Reading, Berkshire became quite flushed when they realized they had been the victims of a hoax. This was due to the fact that the hoaxer had written, in official terms, to many households stating that a member of the Thames Valley Water Board would be standing outside their home monitoring the number of times they flushed their toilet. According to the letter the victims received, the object of the exercise was to identify those householders who used the toilet too often. The offenders were to be threatened with the possibility that their house would have a special water meter installed and that they would have to pay extra because they visited the toilet too frequently.

This hoax proved so successful that eventually the Water Board had to write to all the householders in the area to explain that the whole thing was a joke.

What's Wrong with the Engine?

For this gag you will need a handful of metal nuts. Tie them all together with string. When you have a nice bundle use another piece of string to tie them to the front bumper of your victim's motor car.

As soon as the car starts moving the nuts are dragged along the ground making quite a dreadful noise. It will not be long before the driver stops to investigate – but as soon as the car stops so does the noise! When the car starts up again the noise returns. It could be quite some time before the driver discovers the source of this strange noise. He may even take the car to a garage to have the problem rectified – and it will make the mechanic scratch his head for a while as well!

RATTLE

Man Eating Fish

Make a notice:

MAN EATING FISH
THE WONDER OF THE AGE
MUST BE SEEN TO BE BELIEVED
ENTRANCE ONLY 10p

Put the notice outside your front door and stand by to collect the money. When your victims have all paid up to see the man eating fish take them into the kitchen where your dad is having his fish and chips. 'There you are. A man eating fish!'

This is a good prank for school fêtes as you can use it to make a useful contribution to the school funds.

It Really Happened . . .

In the Royal Scottish Museum, Edinburgh, there is displayed a most unusual stuffed fish. According to the label on the mounting the fish is a fur-bearing trout. This fantastic fish was apparently caught in Lake Superior, one of the Great Lakes between the USA and Canada. The label also states that: 'It is believed that the great depth and the extreme penetrating coldness of the water in which these fish live has caused them to grow their dense coat of (usually) white fur.'

The fur-bearing trout was stuffed and mounted by Ross Jobe, a taxidermist in Marie, Ontario, Canada. But the fish is a fake and it has been reported that Ross Jobe sold over 5000 specimens of this remarkable creature. All he had to do to produce these strange fish was to pin a real fish to a board and then cover the carcass with rabbit fur. In spite of the fact that he advertised these fish as genuine hand-made fakes people flocked to buy them – and no doubt many of the purchasers still believed them to be genuine. So great was his reputation that the Department of Fish and Game in California once asked him for the official biological name of the species!

Scratch It

In most joke shops it is possible to buy itching powder. When it is put down someone's back it makes them itch, just as the name suggests. But it is not absolutely necessary to go to a joke shop to get itching powder. All you need to do is to go out into the British countryside in the autumn. Among the hedgerows you will see the bright red fruits, or hips, of the dog rose. If you open up one of these hips you will find a fluffy substance inside. Pull this out and keep it.

When you put some of this rose-hip fluff down someone's back it will not be very long before he or she starts to itch.

Wrap It Up

This is a very old joke but it is still a good one. At Christmas or on his birthday you give your victim a lovely present. When he removes the covering paper he finds another layer of paper underneath. This is removed only to reveal another layer. Beneath that is another layer, then another, then another and so it goes on and on and on. By the time your friend reaches his present (if there is one in the package) he will be almost buried in paper.

It takes a lot of time and patience to prepare a parcel like this, but as you watch your victim removing layer after layer of paper you will decide that it is well worth the effort.

It Really Happened . . .

A phantom traffic-warden was the creator of an amazing hoax in Maidstone, Kent in 1976. The phoney traffic-warden issued fake parking tickets to many motorists in the town. There were many complaints about the tickets, but these arose not because of the tickets themselves but because they bore abusive language. At the time the Maidstone police were completely baffled. 'We have no idea who is responsible for these fake tickets,' they admitted.

The Ghost Walks

Drape a white sheet over yourself and you will be transformed into a ghost. It can be very scary to see such a ghost in the middle of the night!

To make your ghost even more eerie make some ghostly moans and rattle a piece of chain.

If you have the nerve you could even go out in the street in your ghostly garb. But be careful that you do not meet a real ghost!

Give Us a Ring

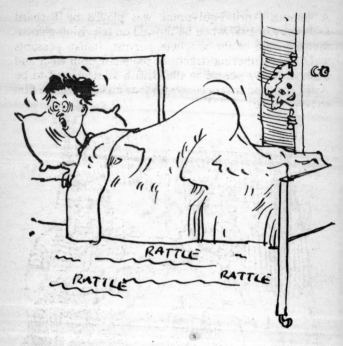

For this prank you need several small bells. The sort used on baby harnesses are ideal, or you may have some among your Christmas tree decorations.

Tie the bells in various places to the springs under your victim's bed. He will wonder where the noise is coming from when he gets into bed. And every time he moves one or more of the bells will ring.

It Really Happened . . .

A famous April Fool prank was played by Richard Dimbleby in 1957 when he showed on television a documentary film of the spaghetti harvest. Italian peasants were seen gathering strands of spaghetti from trees and bushes. Many people in the British Isles proved to be April Fools on that occasion for they all believed the film to be genuine.

Wooden Chocolate

Save the wrapper from your favourite chocolate bar. Now cut a block of wood to exactly the same size as the chocolate. Paint the block of wood chocolate brown. If you want to be really clever you could dip the wood into a saucepan of melted chocolate. Get your mother to do this for you as she will know how to melt the chocolate.

Wrap your wooden chocolate bar in the wrapper you saved.

Next time you buy a bar of chocolate offer the trick one to a friend. When he takes a bite you had better get ready to run away!

It Really Happened . . .

A favourite practical joke of the American prankster Hugh Troy was to buy a wooden bench from a shop and then take it to a nearby park. He and a friend then sat on the bench until they saw a policeman approaching. As soon as the policeman came in sight the two men picked up the bench and ran for their lives. Naturally the policeman assumed they had stolen the bench and chased after them.

It was not until they had been arrested and charged that Troy would gleefully produce the receipt for the bench to prove that he owned it legally.

Chalk Conceit

You announce that you have amazing magical powers. Among your fantastic repertoire is the baffling feat of passing a chalk drawing through a solid object.

To prove this claim you first show your left palm to be completely clean. You then place your left hand beneath the table top.

Now you take a piece of coloured chalk and you draw a small cross on the top of the table. You cover the cross with your right hand. After suitable magical incantations you remove your left hand from beneath the table – there is a coloured cross on it. When you lift your right hand from the table the cross drawn there earlier has completely disappeared. It must have passed clean through the solid top!

To achieve this miracle all you do is draw a small cross on one of the fingernails of your left hand in secret. When this hand is examined later everyone will be looking at the palm and no one will think to turn the hand over.

As soon as your left hand is underneath the table bend your fingers into the palm and press hard. This will transfer the cross from your nail and on to the palm. Open the hand and remove it from beneath the table.

All attention is on the cross on the left palm so it is very easy for you to rub out the cross on the table with your right hand.

To everyone watching it appears that the cross has gone right through the table.

Chair Lift

This is a good prank for parties, but to do it you will need the help of one of your friends.

Ask someone to stand on a chair. That person is then blindfolded. You and your accomplice stand on either side of the chair with your hands holding the chair seat as shown in the illustration.

The victim is told to place one hand on your shoulder and the other hand on your friend's shoulder.

You now explain that you are going to lift the chair. Both you and your accomplice then bend your knees and lower your bodies. Although the victim has not moved he will receive the impression of being lifted up.

Now dare him to jump to the floor while still blindfolded. When he refuses to do so have him remove his blindfold and he will see that the floor is not so far away as he thought it was!

Crazy Purse

When you go into a shop to buy something take this special purse with you and everyone will think you are absolutely crazy. You remove a purse from your pocket and open it to take out some money. Suddenly the purse transforms itself into a sock!

To make this crazy purse you will need a purse frame. This you can obtain from an old purse or you can buy a frame from most shops that sell needlework or craft supplies. You will have to find a frame that is more or less the same size as the top of the sock you are going to use.

Sew the top of the sock around the purse frame and then roll the sock up. Provided that you keep the rolled-up sock to the rear of your crazy purse it will look almost ordinary – until you allow the sock to unroll!

You could even keep your money in this crazy purse. Put it right down in the foot part before rolling the sock up. The weight of the coins will make the sock unroll more quickly. You will look very funny putting your hand right down to the bottom of the sock to get your cash!

Money Stuck

This is a very old joke, but it is still a good one. With some very strong glue stick a coin on the pavement. Now move a short distance away to where you can see the coin but no one can see you. Now wait. Sooner or later someone will spot the coin and try to pick it up. But no matter how hard they try they will not succeed and you will have a good laugh at their antics.

The higher the value of the coin the more effective this joke will be. But do not forget that once the joke is over you will not be able to pick up the coin either. It could turn out to be a very expensive joke if you are not careful.

It Really Happened . . .

Gluing a coin or a £1 note to the pavement as described on the previous page was one of the favourite pranks of Britain's greatest practical joker Horace de Vere Cole.

Another of the many jokes he pulled on the people of Britain involved a length of measuring tape. He would stand near a corner with the tape in his hand and wait for a suitable victim to come along. Explaining that he was a surveyor and that he had to measure around the corner Cole would persuade the victim to hold one end of the tape.

He then disappeared around the corner to persuade another equally gullible victim to hold the other end of the tape. Cole would then retire to a safe place to watch the reactions of the two people when they discovered that they had been tricked.

Foaming Sugar

From your local supermarket buy a jar of liver salts.

Next time you have friends for tea pour the salts into an empty sugar bowl. If your friends are not too observant they will not notice that the sugar looks a little different from usual. To prevent anyone from noticing you could always offer the 'sugar' around yourself, but make sure you keep the bowl just above the eyeline of the person you are serving.

As soon as anyone puts a spoonful of sugar into their cup it will cause their tea to fizz and froth up in a most alarming manner!

Hunting the Gowk

If you fall for an All Fools' Day trick in Scotland you will be called a *gowk*, a word derived from the Icelandic word *gaukr*, meaning 'cuckoo'.

A popular joke in Scotland was to send someone on a fool's errand such as being asked to buy a left-handed tea cup, or to take a message to someone who did not exist. Some suitable errands are given on the next page.

This used to be known as 'hunting the gowk' or, in other words, being sent on a wild goose chase!

Plastic Ice

For this dodge you need some clear plastic. Get an adult to cut it into cubes for you. These cubes should be the same size as the ice cubes you use at home.

Next time you have some friends around for a refreshing drink of fruit juice put some of these plastic ice cubes in the glasses – and then sit back and watch the puzzled reactions of your friends when they discover that the 'ice' does not melt!

It Really Happened . . .

When Christian Morin, president of the French football club Rouen, received a telephone call from Santos, the top Brazilian team, he was absolutely delighted. Santos had offered to play Rouen in a friendly match for £500, a fraction of their normal fee. Morin agreed immediately, for it would be a great boost to his second division football club to have such a famous team on their pitch.

On the day of the match in September 1974 it poured with rain but it did not deter 2000 fans from going to the stadium. They knew their team would lose, but they did not want to miss the opportunity of seeing the great Brazilian footballers in action.

After only a few minutes of play Rouen scored the first goal. It came as quite a surprise. It was assumed that the French team were just lucky because they were more used to playing in the muddy conditions. But then Rouen scored another goal, then another, and another! The Brazilian team were nowhere near as good as had been anticipated. It also seemed rather strange that they shouted to one another in French and not Portuguese. By the end of the match, with Rouen the winners by ten goals to nil, it was obvious that Christian Morin had been hoaxed. He immediately called the police, but by the time they arrived the Brazilian team, in reality a group of hoaxers from Belgium, had disappeared – and taken the £500 with them.

The Abominable Snowman

This joke is best done when there is snow on the ground. The same idea works equally well, however, on mud or sand.

In addition to the snow you will need two plastic buckets and a stick. Put the stick in your pocket and the buckets on your feet.

If you now hold the handle of each bucket you will find it fairly easy to walk. As you walk across the snow you will leave large round prints in the snow. Stop after each step and use the stick to draw enormous claw marks at the front of each print.

Now rush indoors and tell your mother you have just seen the famous abominable snowman. The footprints are proof that some terrible monster has walked across your garden.

Coin Catch

Use some very strong glue to fix some coins to a piece of cardboard. Now glue some more coins on top of the first ones. When the glue has dried cut away any excess cardboard so that it will not be seen when the solid pile of coins is placed down on a table.

In making this pile of coins do not put them on top of one another neatly. The whole idea is that the finished article should look just like a pile of coins that have been placed down casually.

Leave the pile of coins in full view and sooner or later someone will go to pick up one of the coins. They will get quite a shock for all the other coins will come up too!

When you have caught all your friends you will find that this joke pile of coins comes in very handy as a paperweight.

One word of warning: be very careful when using any strong glue. Do not get it on your fingers or on your mother's best furniture or you will be the one to get caught!

Noises in the Night

Buy some dried peas from your local supermarket. You will also need an empty biscuit tin or a metal tray and an empty yoghurt carton or something similar.

Place the tin in your victim's bedroom. Put the yoghurt carton in the tin and fill it with dried peas. Just before your victim goes to bed pour some hot water on the peas.

The hot water soaks into the peas causing them to expand. As a result they begin to be pushed from the cup and make quite a noise as they fall out into the tin. Your victim will think his bedroom is haunted!

For best results the tin should be raised above the ground. A lump of plasticine or a small block of wood at each corner will be suitable for this. The noises will also be louder if the peas have a long way to fall. An easy way to accomplish this is to glue a second yoghurt carton, upside down, to the base of the first so you have a container like the one shown in the illustration.

Have Your Cake and Eat It

If you are at a coffee bar, restaurant, or café with friends, here is a stunt you can try. Let us suppose that one of your friends has bought himself a large cream cake. You would like that cake for yourself but they are rather expensive. This is what you do. Say to your friend: 'I bet you two pence that I could eat that cake without any of it touching my lips or my teeth.'

It sounds such an incredible claim that your friend is very likely to take you up on it. You then eat his cake in the normal way. 'Hey!' he protests, 'it *did* touch your lips and your teeth!'

'Yes, I'm afraid that I have lost the bet. Here is your two pence.'

You may have lost the bet but you have just had a delicious cake for only two pence – and you had better get out of the place quick before your friend realizes how he has been tricked!

Creeping Caterpillars

Cut a pipe cleaner into short pieces. Each piece should be one to two inches (2½ to 5 centimetres) long. Now paint each piece to look like a caterpillar. Do not forget to put in the eyes.

When the paint has dried bend each caterpillar into a wriggly shape.

Now drop them on to a lettuce leaf in a salad, or put them just inside someone's bed – and wait for your victims to scream! Eeek!

It Really Happened . . .

During a military parade the French emperor Napoleon Bonaparte presented a magnificent baton to one of his marshals. The marshal, who was renowned for his conceit, proudly marched up and down the parade ground displaying his new baton. But before very long his pride had turned to bewilderment as the baton began to bend and started melting in the hot sun! Napoleon, who was now laughing heartily at the marshal's downfall, had made the baton out of wax!

The Shrunken Head

Peel a large cooking apple. Now carve the apple into the shape of a human head. You do not have to be very artistic to do this carving as long as you make sure that all the features are included. Don't forget the ears!

Now leave the apple to dry out in a warm place. As it dries it will also shrink and before very long your 'head' will look very gruesome indeed.

When the apple has dried out stick some hair on to it. Real hair is best.

Now take the apple to school and tell everyone it is the head of a friend who was caught by the head-hunters of Borneo. You never know, some of them may believe you!

The Phantom Cat

If you own a violin or if you can borrow one from a friend you can try this prank.

Tie a long length of string to a door handle. To the other end of the string you attach a reasonably heavy weight. Put plenty of rosin on about three feet (just under one metre) of the string. Place the violin on a table underneath the resined length. Now shut the door.

When someone opens the door the weight will pull the string over the violin and produce quite an eerie sound. It is especially scary at night.

Telephone Call

Dial the number for the speaking clock or for any of the recorded telephone services. Now go and tell your mother she is wanted on the telephone.

This is particularly effective if she happens to be in the bath at the time, for she will have to answer the telephone whilst she is still dripping wet. And after all that the 'urgent message' was simply the right time!

It Really Happened . . .

In 1976, during a radio interview, the famous astronomer Patrick Moore invited listeners to take part in a scientific experiment. He said that the planet Pluto was about to pass behind Jupiter and this would exert an increased gravitational pull on the Earth. He told listeners that this would make everyone lighter and that if they jumped up in the air they would float.

As a result people all over Britain began jumping in the air! Many telephoned the BBC to say that what Patrick Moore had said was absolutely true. One caller insisted that he had floated so high that he had hit his head on the ceiling!

Keep It Up

You tell your friend you are going to show him something very interesting. Then you place a chair in the centre of the room and stand on it. This enables you to position a glass of water against the ceiling. You then place one end of a stick against the base of the glass. By holding only the stick you can hold the glass in position against the ceiling.

Now you say to your victim: 'Could you just hold the stick while I get down?' When he has hold of the stick you get down from the chair, move the chair well out of reach and then say, 'Good-bye'. The victim dare not move for if he does the glass of liquid will fall!

A Pocketful of Lemonade

For this joke you will need to fit a plastic lining into one of your jacket pockets. Girls, who may not have a suitable pocket, could use a purse or a handbag. Fix the lining in position with sticky tape and you are ready to go.

Go into a café and order a glass of lemonade (or whatever you drink normally). Now as casually as you can, say to the person who served you: 'Oh, on second thoughts, I will drink it later.' As you say this you calmly pour the drink into your pocket! You will receive some most astonished looks as a result of this strange action and you can have quite a laugh at the reaction you have brought about.

There are two points to remember when using this gag: the first is not to do a somersault after your performance; the other is to make sure that you pour the drink into the correct (lined) pocket.

Liquid In a Comic

As a change from the previous joke you could pour the drink into a comic. All you have to do is to tape the plastic bag to one of the pages in your comic. As with the last joke you simply pour the liquid directly into the secret pocket. You can open the pages of the comic quite easily but please remember you cannot turn the comic upside down.

It Really Happened . . .

A great hoo-haa was created by a hoax in 1835 when it was announced that the famous English astronomer Sir John Herschel had discovered that men lived on the moon. According to the *New York Sun* these lunar men lived in caves and had long wings sprouting from their shoulders. These amazing revelations had apparently come about because the scientist was testing a powerful new telescope in South Africa. It was reported that this telescope was so powerful that in addition to showing that men lived on the moon it also revealed there were oceans, animals, birds and vegetation on the lunar surface.

But when the Department of Commerce decided that it ought to publish a paper in a scientific journal on the subject it suddenly became apparent that the author, Adams Locke, had written the whole article as a hoax!

Your Shirt Is On Fire

Go up to a friend in a panic and say excitedly: 'Your shirt-tail is on fire!'

Before he has time to think about it, pull the back of his shirt out from his trousers. Then say: 'Don't worry. It's *out* now.'

If he is bigger than you run away as fast as you can.

The Last Straw

With a pin make two holes right through a drinking straw. Each hole should be about two inches (five centimetres) from either end of the straw.

Anyone who uses the straw for drinking will only suck up air.

If you have the patience you could prepare a whole box of straws in this manner. But do not worry, you will still be able to use the straws yourself for drinking. All you have to do is place your fingers on the holes at the top end of the straw.

Raining Confetti

On a rainy day go into a cloakroom and pour some confetti inside every closed up umbrella you can find. When the owners open their umbrellas later in the day they will be showered with confetti – quite embarrassing if they open the umbrella in a crowded street!

It Really Happened . . .

Some people go to enormous lengths to put a practical joke into action. American cinema-owner Sid Grauman once hired a theatre full of wax dummies to fool his friend Jesse Lasky.

Lasky, who was one of the pioneers of the cinema, readily accepted when he was invited to speak before a group of film executives. He was well known for his witty speeches, but somehow this one did not seem to go too well. Not one of his jokes received even the slightest giggle.

At the end of his allotted hour Lasky found out the reason for this unusual lack of response – his audience was composed entirely of wax dummies!

What's On TV?

If your parents regularly buy the *Radio Times* and the *TV Times* you could try this on them. Get the current copy of one of the magazines and carefully remove the staples from the spine. You can now remove the contents from the cover. Next, replace the contents with those taken from the previous week's magazine. You will need a stapling machine to put these into the magazine if you are not to arouse anyone's suspicions. When someone comes to look up the television programmes they will find that all the programmes are different from those advertised!

An alternative method is to put the contents of the *Radio Times* inside the *TV Times* and vice versa.

The same gag can be worked with your friends' comics. In fact any magazine can be used to pull the prank. If you do not have a stapler you can always try the same thing with your father's newspaper. But do not tell him who gave you the idea.

It Really Happened . . .

On 1 April 1971 HRH Prince Charles fooled his fellow students at RAF Cranwell. He announced over the public address system in a disguised voice that there was a fault in the heels of the shoes being worn by officers. All wearers of these shoes were to hand them in to the porter's lodge to be checked – and they all fell for the joke!

Tissue Trick

Many houses these days have boxes of tissues in them. If you have some in your house or you know that there are some in a friend's house you can try this trick.

Carefully remove all the tissues from the box. Separate the tissues one by one. Now place a small spot of glue on each tissue and glue it to the next one. Replace all the tissues in the box.

The next person to pull a tissue from the box is in for a shock – for all the tissues come out together in one long string!

If you want to do this to a friend's tissues the easiest way is to buy a box of tissues of the type he or she normally uses. You make this up in the way described above and then substitute your box for theirs at a convenient moment.

Dribble It!

With a pin make several small holes just below the rim of a paper cup. Pour some lemonade into the cup and hand it to a friend. When he drinks from the cup the lemonade will dribble out through the holes and all over your poor unfortunate victim!

The Horrible Handshake

You need to wear gloves for this joke. The left-hand glove is worn in the normal way but that on the right hand is specially prepared.

Fill the glove with newspaper, tissues, or material. Make sure that the padding goes right down into the finger-tips. It should look as if there is a hand in the glove.

Now pull your right arm up your sleeve. Position the stuffed glove in the end of your right sleeve. The fingers of your right hand hold the top of the glove to stop it from falling from the sleeve.

Next time you shake hands with a friend use this stuffed glove. As you shake hands let go of the glove. Your friend will receive quite a shock when your hand falls off.

It Really Happened . . .

Hugh Troy, who is mentioned elsewhere in this book, never missed any opportunity for a joke. On one occasion in Manhattan, he happened to come across a group of workmen digging a hole in the ground. Almost without thinking he immediately pretended to be a supervisor from the works' head office. He instructed the men to down tools at the site and to dig another hole else-where – a hole that was completely unnecessary!

Snakes Alive!

A gruesome snake that leaps out at your victim when he or she opens something can provide quite a laugh – for you, although maybe not for your poor unfortunate victim!

The main thing you will need to make this joke snake is a spring. This can be bought from a hardware shop but if you know someone who is a keen mechanic he may give you one for nothing. It should not be very strong for you must be able to compress it right down.

Cover the spring with a tube of brightly coloured material and then sew up each end. Do not worry too much if you are not very good at sewing for no one is going to notice. You now have a snake that will give your friends quite a surprise.

Your snake can be hidden in all manner of unlikely places provided that it is held compressed until your victim releases it by opening whatever it is hidden in. If it is a friend's birthday, put the snake in a box and wrap it up as a present. That will prove to be a birthday he will not forget for a long time to come!

Another good hiding place might be a tin your mother is likely to use in the kitchen. Or, if your father takes a lunchbox to work he would get quite a fright when the snake jumps out. But make sure you are not around when your dad comes home, for he may not think the joke is quite as funny as you do! You could even put your snake in your teacher's desk. With a bit of luck he may be so frightened that he will cancel all lessons for the rest of the week!

Ugh! A Spider!

How would you like to have a big, horrible spider to scare people with? Such a spider can create a great deal of fun and it is easy to make.

One way to make your spider is to buy some oasis foam from your local florists (it is used in flower arranging). Cut the foam into the shape of an egg. This is going to be the body of your spider.

Dye eight pipe cleaners black and then push them into the sides of the foam. Bend them to look like legs.

If you would like to have a nice furry spider glue cotton wool, dyed to whatever colour you fancy, all over the body.

For the eyes use map pins or ordinary pins – just push them in at the appropriate place. With all the pin-heads close together a very effective eye can be made. Alternatively you could make eyes from coloured paper or buttons and just glue them on.

Now push a bent pin into the top of the body to act as a hook. Tie a bit of black cotton to the hook and you can dangle your spider wherever you like.

It is also worth making another hook from a paper-clip. Hang this on a light shade as shown in the illustration and pass the thread over it. By pulling the end of the thread you can make the spider go up and down in the most scarey manner.

Another way to make the spider mobile is to hook the thread to a picture rail. The other end of the thread is fixed at floor level by tying it around the leg of a chair. Hang the spider at the top end of the thread and let go as someone walks into the room. The spider will zoom down the thread and provide quite a fright to whoever has just entered.

It Really Happened . . .

When the politician Oliver Locker-Lampson stated that a Member of Parliament could not be arrested, it was too much of a temptation to the great British practical joker Horace de Vere Cole. He resolved to have the politician inside a prison cell before the day was out.

He challenged Locker-Lampson to a race along a London street. The politician accepted the challenge, but he was so keen for the race to start that he did not notice Cole slip his watch into the MP's pocket. The race started and Cole deliberately let the other man take the lead. He then shouted at the top of his voice 'Stop thief!' and chased after the astounded politician.

The police promptly gave chase and arrested Locker-Lampson. He protested his innocence but the fact that Cole's watch was found in his pocket proved irrefutable evidence and he was taken into custody. Only then did Horace de Vere Cole reveal that the whole episode had been a practical joke!

Bleeding Finger

This is a useful dodge for getting out of any work you do not wish to do. It is also a handy way of receiving sympathy and of gaining a reputation of being brave because even though you are badly wounded you manage to carry on in spite of the great pain you are in (at least, that is what other people will think).

What people do not realize is that the blood-stained bandage you have on your finger is a fake. You make it by first putting a strip of thin card around your finger and then gluing it in position. Now bandage the finger over the card – do not forget to take the bandage over the end of the finger. Tie the bandage and then use some red ink or paint to make a gory blood stain on the top of the bandage as shown in the illustration.

Because of the paper inside, this fake bandage can be slipped on and off your finger quite easily. Do not let anyone see you put it on or the game will be up. And don't forget to groan occasionally to show your intense pain!

Obstinate Thread

Tie a few knots together in a piece of cotton so that they form one large knot. This knot should be about four inches (10 centimetres) from one end. Thread the other end of the thread on to a needle and push this through your coat from the outside to the inside. Pull the thread inside your coat until the knot prevents it from going any further. It will look as if there is a loose piece of thread on your coat.

Cut the end of thread which is inside your jacket so it hangs just above the bottom of the coat. Tie a weight to this end of the thread. This weight can be a key or a coin with a hole in it – anything you have handy.

Now put your coat on and wait for someone to notice the loose piece of thread. When it is drawn to your attention you pull it out until you are holding the thread at arm's length. Now let go and the weight will cause the thread to fly back into the coat leaving the same short piece showing. The knot, of course, stops it from going right inside the coat.

If someone tries to remove the thread themselves, simply move backwards slightly until the thread is fully extended. Take the thread from the other person and then let it go.

It looks very funny to see the thread going back into the coat of its own accord.

It Really Happened . . .

After a day's work during the filming of 'Buffalo Bill and the Indians' actor Paul Newman returned to his location caravan for a rest. As he opened the door he was almost drowned in a sea of popcorn that flooded out. The film's director, Robert Altman, had filled the caravan from top to bottom with popcorn!

Newman got his own back by filling Altman's caravan with 300 live chickens! He then sent out thousands of invitations to a party at the director's home – a party that did not exist.

Pop-up Toothpaste

You will have to search around for the things you will need for this joke but it will be well worth the effort. The first item is easy enough to come by for it is simply an empty toothpaste tube. You will also need a metal tube with a small enough diameter to fit through the nozzle of the tube and of such a length that it will be hidden completely in the tube. In addition you will need a small spring to fit inside the metal tube, and a length of wooden dowelling that also fits into the tube.

Put the spring into the metal tube and then insert this into the toothpaste tube. Now put in the dowelling (it is as well to paint this white) and push it down against the spring. Put the cap on the toothpaste and then place the tube in your bathroom.

When someone opens the toothpaste the dowelling will pop up and give them quite a fright!

108

This is not the beginning.
Got you fooled, didn't we?

A GHOST HUNTER'S HANDBOOK

Peter Underwood

Long-time ghost expert and hunter, Peter Underwood, tells children all they need to know about ghosts, their habits and habitats. Peter Underwood, who is president of the Ghost Club and copyright holder of the only known photograph of a ghost, has written several books on ghosts for adults, but this is his first book on the subject for children. Serious in approach, it covers everything from how to find a ghost to information on ghosts that have been found in all parts of the world, and includes a section on famous ghosts and haunted houses that can be visited.

85p

The Sparrow Bookshop

Sparrow has a whole nestful of exciting books that are available in bookshops or that you can order by post through the Sparrow Bookshop. Just complete the form below and enclose the money due and the books will be sent to you at home.

☐ BERTHA AND THE RACING PIGEON	Pam Ayres	85p
☐ THE SPUDDY	Lillian Beckwith	85p
☐ THE JELLYBONE GRAFFITI BOOK	Therese Birch	85p
☐ THE BIRTHDAY KITTEN	Enid Blyton	70p
☐ MIDSHIPMAN BOLITHO	Alexander Kent	80p
☐ THE PONY SEEKERS	Diana Pullein-Thompson	85p
☐ THE CHILDREN'S GARDENING BOOK	John Seymour	90p
☐ WORZEL GUMMIDGE AND THE TREASURE SHIP	Barbara E. Todd	85p

Picture books

☐ IF MICE COULD FLY	John Cameron	£1.25
☐ NOT NOW, BERNARD	David McKee	£1.25
☐ K9 AND THE MISSING PLANET	David Martin	65p
	Total plus postage	

And if you would like to hear more about our forthcoming books, write to the address below for the Sparrow News.

SPARROW BOOKS, BOOKSERVICE BY POST, PO BOX 29, DOUGLAS, ISLE OF MAN, BRITISH ISLES

Please enclose a cheque or postal order made out to Arrow Books Limited for the amount due including 8p per book for postage and packing for orders within the UK and 10p for overseas orders.

Please print clearly

NAME _____

ADDRESS _____

_____

Whilst every effort is made to keep prices down and popular books in print, Arrow Books cannot guarantee that prices will be the same as those advertised here or that the books will be available.